What's Worth Fighting For?

What's Worth Fighting For in the Principalship?
SECOND EDITION

Michael Fullan

Coming Soon:

What's Worth Fighting For in Your School?
SECOND EDITION

Andy Hargreaves and Michael Fullan

What's Worth Fighting For in Educational Change?
SECOND EDITION

Michael Fullan and Andy Hargreaves

What's Worth Fighting For in the Principalship?

SECOND EDITION

Michael Fullan

Teachers College
Columbia University
New York and London

ONTARIO
PRINCIPALS'
COUNCIL
Exemplary Leadership
in Public Education

Published simultaneously by Teachers College Press, 1234 Amsterdam Avenue, New York, NY 10027 and by the Ontario Principals' Council, 180 Dundas Street West, Toronto, Ontario, Canada, M5G 1Z8

Library of Congress Cataloging-in-Publication Data

Fullan, Michael.
    What's worth fighting for in the principalship? / Michael Fullan. — 2nd ed.
        p. cm.
    Includes bibliographical references.
    ISBN 978-0-8077-4833-6 (pbk. : alk. paper)
        1. Elementary school principals. I. Title.
    LB2831.6.F85   2008
    372.12′012—dc22   2007046964

ISBN 978-0-8077-4833-6 (paper)

Printed on acid-free paper
Manufactured in the United States of America

15 14 13 12 11 10 09 08   8 7 6 5 4 3 2 1

Contents

Preface

This book is a complete rewrite of *What's Worth Fighting For in the Principalship?* Thirty years ago, an official from one of the teacher unions in Ontario came to me and said, "We would like you to write a book that will help our principals" (at the time, principals were members of the union). He said that the principals were complaining that the job was getting worse, demands were greater, it was more and more difficult to get things done, and satisfaction on any given day was hard to come by.

He proceeded to say that we will give you the title and three criteria. The title is "What's Worth Fighting For in the Principalship?" The criteria are: (1) write something that is deeply insightful, (2) make sure it contains lots of practical-action advice, and, (3) above all, be concise. Indeed! For an academic, this was a challenge. If you are lucky you might get any two of these, but this tripartite crucible led to a new style of thinking and writing, which has carried over to this day.

The first edition of *What's Worth Fighting For in the Principalship?* (*WWFFP*) was published in 1988. Andy Hargreaves joined me to cowrite *What's Worth Fighting For in Your School?* (*WWFFS*), published in 1991, and *What's Worth Fighting for Out There?* (*WWFFOT*) in 1998. Now, a decade later, it is time to rewrite the trilogy, starting with *WWFFP*.

Much has changed rapidly over the past decade. The *What's Worth Fighting For* trilogy (henceforth: *WWFF*) is about taking relentless action in the face of an amalgam of intersecting barriers and creating powerful levers for catapulting the system forward. Despite the complexity, and in fact because of the interrelatedness of growing complexity, we believe that a small number of powerful interconnected forces *could* result in new breakthroughs in the next short while. One's passions and crafted ingenuity can be especially aroused when fighting for something big that is on the verge of happening—if only it is propelled by the actions we recommend in this trilogy.

These are exciting, difficult, and contentious times, and the principal is at dead center in all of it. In the earlier edition of *WWFFP*, the argument was made that the system fosters *dependency* through consistent bombardment of new tasks and continual interruption. I was empathetic (but not sympathetic) to the plight of principals. I argued that there was no point in waiting around for the system to improve, and I urged principals to take charge and to assume that on any given day the system may not know what it is doing.

Great advice still, but the situation has become much more complex. The good news is that, finally, the principalship is being recognized by politicians and policymakers as key to student learning, especially in raising the bar and closing the achievement gap for all students. The bad news is that these policymakers have overloaded the ship with a cross-cutting cacophony of expectations that serve only to hinder deep action. The irony is that, at the same time that the principal has been elevated and viewed as critical to success, the principalship itself is sinking—overloaded and pulled down.

In this book, I seek a way out of the current dilemma. I am interested in helping incumbent and would-be principals leverage action that will change the system positively in small and large ways. I am also concerned about how the *system* can get it right, acting, so to speak, as if it *did* know what it is doing.

For this transformation to occur, both the principal and the system have a responsibility to unlock the potential of what has become a pivotal but unrealized force for change—the school principal in the 21st century. I say "potentially" because the power of the principal is currently locked in a vise-like grip of frustrated inertia, at the very time when the moral core of society is in jeopardy.

In Chapter 1, I start with the *vise* principal, showing how the principalship is being shackled at the same time that the principal is expected to be the lead change agent. I show that the solution is not to free the principals to be autonomous saviors of the day. *Interdependence* is the core concept. The essential themes of the interdependent solutions are contained in Chapters 2 through 5. Principals need to lead every day in making short-term headway as "leading legacies" of the next generation of leaders (Chapter 2). In this overloaded information age they need to "lead knowledgeably" (Chapter 3). They need to spawn, harness, and "lead learning communities" within and beyond the school—with parents, community agencies, and educators alike (Chapter 4). In an exciting way, principals are in a position to help "lead system change" (Chapter 5). The action implications are distilled in a set of guidelines in Chapter 6.

WWFFP has always had a bias for action. What is significant about this edition is that everything I talk about is based on named, actual examples. There is nothing remote, abstract, or inaccessible about the ideas. They are all grounded in action.

I believe we are now in a position to engage together in insightful action. Learning by doing is as much about the mind and the heart as it is about the action itself. But you have to be in the midst of the battle to stir mindful emotions in effective directions. None are better positioned than principals to surround themselves with a million change agents. Only that will get the job done, which is to establish conditions, cultures, and commitment on a large scale and to engage in continuous improvement—if you will pardon the redundancy—*all the time.*

My thanks especially to Andy Hargreaves, who provided insightful feedback on *WWFFP*, and who will coauthor the second and third books of the trilogy. Andy is a constructive, critical, generous person to have as a coauthor and friend. He always sharpens the debate and insights in anything we do together. To Teachers College Press and the Ontario Principals' Council, thank you for being great editors. My thanks especially to Carole Saltz, Publisher of TC Press, for her unfailing support over the years. Thanks also to Lynda Mason, who produced the manuscript with great quality and in a very short time. My deep appreciation to Claudia Cuttress for her contribution to all the projects we do. Finally, thanks to all the principals who are working to elevate the leadership of schools—a moral contribution of the highest order.

What's Worth Fighting For in the Principalship?

SECOND EDITION

CHAPTER 1

The *Vise* Principal

What's new for the principal? Powerful changes forces have certainly bombarded the principalship, making life more onerous, but also containing glimpses of new interdependent components. I see eight high-magnitude change forces at play; the first four being problematic and the last four being mixtures of downsides and elements of great potential:

1. Initiativitis
2. High-stakes vulnerability
3. Managerial diversions
4. Unfit for purpose
5. Strategies with potential
6. Recruitment and succession
7. Clusters, networks, and partnerships
8. International benchmarks

PROBLEMATIC CHANGE FORCES

1. Initiativitis

Initiativitis is the tendency to launch an endless stream of disconnected innovations that no one could possibly manage. In *Change Without Pain*, Abrahamson (2004) calls this the "repetitive change syndrome": "The symptoms? Initiative overload, change-related chaos and widespread employee anxiety, cynicism and burnout" (p. 2).

In the United States, the Wallace Foundation's (2003) major ongoing work on "leadership for learning" captures the same phenomenon. Noting lack of coherence in leadership policies and practices, they summarize:

> The most common results of a fragmented, disconnected system of school leadership are: state, district and school policies and practices that are out of synch and even at odds; a perennial search for superhero leaders who are, by definition, in short supply; . . . and a climate where effective practices are rarely documented or shared, how progress is limited to single teachers, classrooms or schools, and where successes are not institutionalized so they survive after the superhero leaves. (p. 5)

Referring to a national survey, the Wallace Group reports that "54 percent of superintendents and 48 percent of principals believe that they need to work around the system" to get things done. Fewer than one-third believe that "the system" is on their side (p. 4).

The recent major study of school leadership in England by PriceWaterhouseCoopers (PWC) found the same problem: "the word 'initiativitis' was often used by the leaders we spoke to as a way of expressing their frustration with the number of policy initiatives they were having to deal with, the apparent inconsistencies between them and the lack of resources to deal with them" (2007, p. vii). It is interesting to note that PWC had limited sympathy for the situation, observing that "it seemed to us to reflect a wish for stability and consistency which cannot be delivered and which is not enjoyed by any other organization in the public or private sector" (p. vii). There is some truth to this. But no other sector experiences the barrage of externally imposed accountability demands, along with imposed, fragmented innovations (see my next theme). In any case, the solution involves a combination of individual and system correction.

In a survey conducted by Headspace in England, well over 80% of elementary and secondary school heads said that they have had to do more over the last 5 years in "implementation of government initiatives" and "dealing with bureaucracy." Over two-thirds report an increase in "business management of school budget" (cited in PWC, 2007).

There is no question that the role of school leader has become more complex and in many ways "undoable" under current conditions. My solution, as we will see, is not to strive for stability, but to reposition the role of principal so that school leaders can be a force for school *and* system transformation.

2. High-Stakes Vulnerability

One culprit in initiativitis is the accountability scheme that is externally imposed, ill-conceived, and punitively driven. Once again, a sensible idea (accountability to the public) has taken a wrong turn. Big systems have a habit of looking for quick fixes, irrespective of local conditions and motivations.

My colleague Richard Elmore (2004) has made the case more than once that no amount of *external* accountability can succeed in the absence of *internal-to-the-school* accountability. You need both, and developing the capacity for internal accountability (internalizing the values and practices of responsibility and efficacy) must go hand-in-hand with engaging the external accountability system. Otherwise external intervention by itself will result in pro forma compliance and, if anything, spawn practices that prop up short-term test scores in ways that actually harm schools in the mid- to long-term.

Virtually every jurisdiction has accountability-based "turn-around schools" requirements that call for intervention inversely proportionate to success. Using short-term disembodied measures, increasingly bad things happen to low-performing schools. In the United States, accountability components of No Child Left Behind (NCLB), along with the various state derivatives, are disasters of misplaced accountability. Turnaround policies depend heavily on *external* control: a new principal, a plethora of reporting requirements, external consultants, and so forth. Minthrop (2004) captures the perverse phenomenon of high-stakes accountability in which so-called "success" means one baby step forward and one giant leap backward. As he notes, an initial focus on external control can reduce gross deficiencies and reverse the decline of bad scores, but only temporarily. The pressure of probation and the stigma of being "low-performing" have most teachers running scared, and good teachers just running (to greener pastures). In such labeled schools, teachers can either comply or walk. The compliance is superficial and short-term—punitive measures do not instill the will for continuous high performance. One-sided anxiety-producing pressures, says Minthrop, are sometimes avoided with *exit*, "particularly where exit options are abundant, which they are for the more talented teachers" (p. 5). Precisely the opposite must happen: "The best people must be incentivized to work on the worst problems" (Fullan, 2006, p. 52).

3. Managerial Diversion

I favor strong management, just not with the CEO doing it all. The demands for managing budget, plant, personnel, and public relations (complaints) have all increased. The role description of principals includes all of these, along with the expectation to lead instructional improvement, operating from a vise-like position. This is a system problem, but is also aided and abetted by some individual principals. Let's take the latter first. PWC (2007) calls the managerial component of the principal "operations." The PWC evidence suggests that many school leaders are too involved in operational and delivering matters, and that this has been *at the expense of their more strategic imperatives.*

Numerous stories were identified of head teachers unblocking toilets, filling dishwashers, or supervising pupils before and after school. Managerial and strategic overload, as I have said, has increased dramatically in the past 5 years, but this problem is aggravated by "a mindset amongst some school leaders [that] is often more comfortable with an operation role than a strategic one" (PWC, 2007, p. vii). In other words, some school leaders are more comfortable doing the paperwork first, and strategic direction second (if they have time for it, which of course they never do).

I will be recommending later in this book that more resources must be allocated so that principals can hire "business managers" or have assistant principals supported in this role. But they will have to know how to use them, and some of them just don't. This takes us directly to our next barrier: unfit for purpose.

4. Unfit for Purpose

In terms of job expectations, the role of the principal has changed dramatically in the past 3 to 5 years. Whether you believe Ken Leithwood and colleagues' (2004) description of the basic core of the work of school leaders ("building strategic direction, understanding and developing people, redesigning the organization, and managing the teaching and learning program"), or PWC's big six ("strategic direction and ethos, teaching and learning, developing and managing people, networking and collaboration between schools and with other agencies, operations, and accountability"), or PWC's portrayal of "the changing landscape of schools which include: new relationships with schools, the learning environment, the learning and social agency agenda, personalized learning, and partnerships"—there was one undeniable conclusion: The job of the school head is incredibly more complex and *substantially different* from what it was even a short time ago.

There are two problems with this rapid change toward greater complexity. One is that many school principals entered the role with very different expectations from what has turned out to be the case. They have been misled (or have misled themselves) into thinking that they would end up managing the kind of school we all knew, with perhaps major changes in the ethnic composition of the school, but not in management itself. In this sense, they are unfit for the purpose at hand. The other problem is that, with the scarcity of applicants for the principalship and with rapid demographically related turnover, out of necessity many educators are being promoted prematurely to the role. These newcomers are not necessarily ill-fitted to the post, but they do not yet have the experience for the demands they face.

In addition to individuals being unfit, I have argued that the *role* itself as it stands now is not fit for the *purpose*. It can't be done effectively except by superheroes. This becomes a vicious cycle. The role fails to attract enough of the right people and critical masses of strategically effective leaders fail to materialize, thereby further weakening the fostering of distributed leaders. This forces the system to look for superheroes. All and all, the system gets the principals it deserves. This is less an individual failure than it is a failure of the system. Making the reality of the principal's *role* fit for the *purposes* now laid out in England's *Every Child Matters* and the deeper purposes of the U.S. No Child Left Behind Act needs to be a major priority. Fit for purpose *is What's Worth Fighting For in the Principalship*.

PROMISING CHANGE FORCES

The preceding four new themes in the principal's world are just downright bad—bad for the health of individuals, and bad for the health of the system. The remaining four are double-edged. They can be either problematic or potentially powerful, if pursued well and in combination.

5. Strategies with Potential

Think of a strategy to reform urban schools by focusing on literacy, math, and science. Add $35 million of new money. Develop and align world-class standards, curriculum, and instruction to meet those standards, and an assessment system to track and mark progress. Invest heavily in professional development for teachers. Finally, re-establish new proactive leadership roles in the enterprise for school principals, and provide them with plenty of professional development.

Would you expect results? Not according to The Cross City Campaign for Urban School Reform (2005), which studied just such reform initiatives in Chicago, Milwaukee, and Seattle. Their bottom-line conclusion: "the unfortunate reality for many principals and teachers we interviewed is that the districts were unable to change and improve practice on a large scale" (p. 4). As for the principals, they were positioned to play a key role, but "principals had multiple responsibilities that often worked at cross purposes with their role of instructional leaders" (p. 9).

Looking at a study with even more prominence, the principalship was central to the high-profile, highly supported literacy and math reform effort in San Diego in the 1997–2002 period (Hubbard, Mehan, & Stein, 2006). The theory of action envisioned principals as "the most critical resource in the professional guidance and instructional direction of the school" (p. 75). Called on to be "leaders of instruction, principals were to spend more time in classrooms, engaging teachers in conversations about instruction, and to spend less time on administrative, logistical, and financial matters" (p. 5). Despite a relentless focus and lots of on-the-scene mentoring, enormous difficulties were encountered in linking school leadership to instructional improvement across classrooms.

So what is going on here? Policymakers and district leaders finally take research findings on the role of the principal seriously, and they *still* hit a wall? I favor four explanations in combination.

1. Districts are expecting principals to carry out roles that are centrally (district) determined.
2. Maybe the role of instructional leader is far more daunting than people imagined, and cannot be learned through a series of workshops or even via one-on-one mentoring. Learning in context requires that we focus on changing the culture of the school so that educators learn continuously in the setting in which they work.
3. Perhaps principals are constrained by policies and practices on the selection and monitoring of teachers, or on budgets and other aspects of bureaucracy.
4. As we noted earlier, the new expectations have been added to the traditional ones, without any consideration of whether the new role, in its entirety, is feasible under the current working conditions of teachers. The net effect is that the principal is being placed in an impossible position.

Arising from these frustrations is a new wave of strategies. A good example is New York, which (after numerous structural flip-flops in the past decade) is now offering schools one of three alternatives. First, they can choose to be an "authentically empowered" school (New York City Schools, 2006). These schools get fiscal, staffing, and administrative empowerment in exchange for meeting firm accountability requirements. Second, principals can choose a revamped connection with Learning Service Organizations—there are four LSOs from which to choose. Third, they can join a private consortia (commercial and university institutions that bid for contracts to run sets of schools)—a choice that is still in the early stage of development and currently has only nine approved "providers." I won't comment on this latest iteration in detail, save to say that if the strategies do not incorporate the four powerful themes in Chapters 2 through 5, they will surely fail.

A more promising cluster-based set of strategies has been evolving over the past 3 years in England (see Caldwell, 2006, and our Theme 7 on cluster, networks, and partnerships). These new approaches have considerable potential, but require sophisticated theories of action to support them. Andy Hargreaves evaluated just such a project, called "Raising Achievement, Transforming Learning" (RATL) and led by the Specialist Schools and Academies Trust (Hargreaves & Shirley, 2006).

RATL serves more than 300 low-performing secondary schools in England. The theory of action or change model is based on the following six components:

1. Identifies and invites participation by underperforming schools
2. Networks schools together
3. Makes available mentor schools and heads
4. Provides visionary inspiration and motivational network conferences, and, through project leadership, supplies technical systems and assistance in analyzing data and targeting improvement efforts

5. Collects and injects into the network an array of experience-driven and practically proven strategies
6. Incentivizes participation through modest funding

The results are very encouraging. Some three-quarters of the schools have improved significantly in student achievement within just 3 years. Remember that these are all low-performing secondary schools. There are still many challenges, such as addressing the situation of the one-fourth of the schools that have failed to move forward, the need to drill down, how to extend the success to additional schools, how to sustain improvements where they have initially been made, and how to wean schools from focusing only on short-term strategies at the expense of harder-to-get-at longer-term solutions. As with all current solutions, the need is to continually identify and apply specific solutions to specific problems. Specificity and precision tailored to particular conditions and needs is the hallmark of effective change strategies (see Fullan, 2008).

In sum, there is still a preponderance of partially conceived reform strategies that place principals front and center in ways that set them up for failure. But there are glimpses of new approaches that have powerful promise. The good news is that, because all else has failed over the past 2 decades of intensive reform efforts, this is a time of radical experimentation. This opportunity makes the new *WWFFP* action guide especially timely.

6. Recruitment and Succession

It is hard to get a given role correct when both ends of the continuum are ignored. Until recently, recruitment and succession have been almost totally neglected. Of course, it is hard to *recruit* the right people to a bad situation. As we say, "how are you going to keep them down on the farm once they have seen the farm?" Or how are you even going to get them to the farm once they know so much about it? As the Wallace Foundation (2003) leadership report argues, part of the solution involves role clarity and better preparation, but a bigger part involves changing the "conditions and incentives" under which principals work.

You can't just start with the principal. As the success in Finland demonstrates (where all teachers are required to have master's degrees *prior* to entering the teaching force), it starts with a foundational bedrock of quality teachers across the board. Then you can spawn leaders developing other leaders, pipelines of potential future leaders learning leadership in the settings in which they work. And only then will incentives and opportunities to take up the principalship be attractive to teacher leaders.

As for *succession*, Hargreaves and Fink (2006) found that episodic, unplanned succession was the norm. This is especially dispiriting in cases of initial successful turnaround. They discovered that good new work is short-lived because of the absence of any plan to build on it. The outcome is "recent success is discontinued, improvement gains are eliminated, and continuity is reestablished with earlier, more mediocre patterns. [The end result] is a perpetual carousel where schools move up and down with depressing regularity" (p. 71).

At least now major attention is being paid to new schemes for recruitment and succession (see, especially, England's National College of School Leadership, www.ncsl.org.uk). But what goes in the sandwich—the meat, the vegetables, the substance—matters. Recruitment and succession will improve only to the extent that the in-between working conditions are an essential part of the agenda. *What's Worth Fighting For in the Principalship?* is about the whole sandwich! This means combating the vise-related aspects of the eight constraints in this chapter as you rebuild the school system around the four themes in Chapters 2 through 5.

7. Clusters, Networks, and Partnerships

I see clusters, networks, and partnerships as vital to the future of the principalship and to the success of the system as a whole. But like all of the final four themes in this chapter, they can do harm, do nothing, or do good.

Networks can be *time-wasters* if one has to participate in several and/or if they involve superficial exchanges. Networks can serve to shield *school autonomy* in dysfunctional ways as systems like New York move to "authentic empowerment" if the latter is not accompanied by powerful networks of learning across schools. Networks can foster focusing on *narrow* learning agendas based only on short-term test scores, if deeper goals are not explicitly pursued.

The networks or partnerships we envision must be powerful, focused on teams, and concerned with drilling down into deep continuous improvement. The vital success in the RATL projects mentioned above depended on four factors:

1. Improvement by schools, with schools, and for schools
2. Being driven simultaneously by research-based evidence and professional experience and wisdom
3. Engaging in iterative cycles of research and development and vice versa
4. Using and valuing outside-in leadership and expertise, as well as inside-out (to other schools) knowledge

It is going to require a lot of leadership at the school and district levels to get the best out of "lateral capacity building," which, when it works, unleashes two potent change forces: knowledge and more extensive identity and moral commitment. As Caldwell (2006) puts it:

> A feature of successful experience is the conversations that schools and school systems must have with other organizations—public and private—in education and non-education settings. . . . There must be a horizontal network of relationships in addition to a vertical continuum of authority and responsibility. (p. 25)

The world of the school principal is becoming flatter!

8. International Benchmarks

Andy Hargreaves and I have an ongoing debate about the question of "targets" for literacy or other areas. Targets will do harm when they are arbitrary and externally imposed. They will do good in situations with a previous lack of focus and when jointly determined. In the end, we agree that targets are a red herring and not essential—although I would say that schools are better off if they establish aspirational targets (say, in literacy) relative to their starting points.

Two things are essential. One is that schools and school systems reference their progress. The other is that schools generate continuous diagnostic data on the learning and implementation processes they are using in order to inform and refine improvement strategies. With respect to the former, jurisdictions should compare themselves in three ways:

1. Themselves with themselves over time. What is the extent of progress relative to previous performance?
2. Apples with apples. How are they doing in comparison with other schools facing similar circumstances?
3. To some absolute standard. What is the percentage of students achieving proficiency in literacy, both within the local system and compared to international standards?

Regarding the last point, OECD's PISA (Program for International Student Assessment), which assesses the performance of 15-year-olds in the 32-member countries, is a useful benchmark and has generated considerable interest in learning from high-performing nations, such as Finland.

In the meantime, most systems suffer from information overload and are driven to distraction more than to improvement (Shirley & Hargreaves, 2006). The solution is for school leaders to become assessment literate, and for systems to back away from the misuse of data and to move toward provisions of information that will be of service both internally for the school and externally for accountability.

I have found that schools and districts that use student achievement data to inform and mark progress not only become more comfortable with transparent information, they *seek* it. Turnaround strategies, for example, are unsuccessful when they start with the stigma of failure. When these same strategies are nonpejorative, focusing instead on partnerships and capacity-building (such as the RATL project, and the Ontario Focused Intervention Partnership), the entire climate changes. Moral commitment flourishes, knowledge flows, and educators want data that show how they are doing and what they have to work on to get better.

In summary, what we have covered in this chapter are eight powerful themes that have dramatically altered the landscape for school leaders. While ratcheting up expectations to stratospheric levels, these themes also act as a series of vise-like clamps that prevent the principal from really going anywhere.

The solution is not to unfetter the principal to act autonomously, but rather to enable focused cohesion. When it comes to all things social, the metaphor of *webs* is more potent, tough, resilient, and dynamic. Vises are for inanimate objects that you don't want to go anywhere, while you shape them to your liking. Webs are alive. The rest of this book is about four interrelated learning webs and their associated actions—a set well worth fighting for now that the stakes are so high.

CHAPTER 2

Leading Legacies

This book is intended equally for individual principals and for system leaders interested in developing the principalship. Above all, we don't want individuals to wait for the "system" to get its act together. Change never happens that way.

Leading legacies is one area where individuals can make a direct contribution to improving themselves, while simultaneously strengthening the system for the long run. George Bernard Shaw captures this magnificently in *Man and Superman*:

> This is the true joy in life, the being used for a purpose recognized by "yourself as a mighty one"; the being a force of nature instead of a feverish little clod of ailments and grievances complaining that the world will not devote itself to making you happy; I want to be thoroughly used up when I die, for the harder I work the more I live. I rejoice in life for its own sake. Life is no "brief candle" to me. It is a sort of splendid torch which I have got hold of for the moment, and I want to make it burn as brightly as possible before handing it on to future generations. (1903, p. ii)

Leading legacies is about splendid torches that burn forever: School principals lead legacies in four ways:

1. They lead for others.
2. They develop collaborative cultures.
3. They link to the outside.
4. They leave fond memories.

LEADING FOR OTHERS

We know that effective principals have to do two things jointly: to focus deeply on instruction (Chapter 3) and help others do so in the short run, and also especially to put others in a position to carry on beyond the leader's tenure. When there are urgent problems and one is expected as leader to have the answers, there is great temptation to jump in and solve the problem. This is not legacy leading. Ken Leithwood and his colleagues recently completed a study for the National College of School Leadership (NCSL) in England in which they offered "Seven strong claims about successful school leadership" (Leithwood et al., 2007). Two of the these claims bear directly on establishing conditions for legacy:

- School leadership has a greater influence on schools and students when it is widely distributed.
- School leaders improve learning indirectly and most powerfully through their influence on staff motivation, commitment, and working conditions. (p. 3)

Henry Mintzberg, McGill University's iconoclastic business professor, nails the basic case for leaving legacies. He starts with Livingston's 1971 article in the *Harvard Business Review*: "successful managing in Livingston's opinion is not about one's own success but fostering success in others" (Mintzberg, 2004, p. 16).

Later on, Mintzberg elaborates:

Leadership is not about making clever decisions and doing bigger deals, least of all for personal gain. It is about energizing other people to make good decisions and do better things. In other words, it is about helping release the positive energy that exists naturally within people. Effective leadership inspires more than it empowers; it connects more than it controls; it demonstrates more than it decides. It does all this by *engaging*—itself above all, and consequently others. (p. 143; emphasis in original)

As Leithwood and his colleagues say, "school leadership is second only to classroom teaching as an influence on learning" (2007, p. 3). Thus, principals leave legacies by modeling instructional leadership, emphasizing that improving teaching and learning is central, and getting the right teachers to become leaders (literacy coaches, grade-level heads, principal preparation programs).

Effective principals then spend their time creating the conditions for teachers and teacher leaders to zero-in on effective instructional practices, and to use data on student learning both as a lever for improvement and as a source for external accountability.

Incidentally, the best business companies all practice this bedrock principle of leaders developing other leaders (Fullan, 2008). Toyota is one company that builds its success from the inside-out and is based on this premise: "Toyota's philosophy is every team leader and manager is a *teacher* first" (Liker & Meier, 2007, p. 283, emphasis added). And "the biggest success of any manager is the success of the people they have taught" (p. 313).

Interestingly, you don't have to die or retire to leave a legacy. Great leaders develop those around them at a fast rate and in high numbers, so much so that the organization cannot absorb them soon enough. Stated differently, leaders who develop other leaders provide a farm system for other organizations. It may be frustrating to groom internal leaders only to have them leave early for other leadership positions, but in public schools, especially, helping to develop leadership for the system as a whole is an immediate form of legacy leaving.

DEVELOPING COLLABORATIVE CULTURES

In addition to any one-on-one mentoring principals engage in, their greatest contribution comes, indirectly, from the collaborative cultures they create (see also Chapter 4). Leithwood and colleagues (2004) conclude that principals influence student learning by:

1. Setting directions (shared vision and group goals, high performance and expectations)
2. Developing people (individual support, intellectual/ emotional stimulation, modeling)
3. Redesigning the organization (collaborative cultures and structures, building productive relations with parents and the community)

We have known for a quarter-century that focused collaborative cultures generate greater student learning. However, it is only in the past 5 years that this knowledge is being deliberately applied, usually under the label of "professional learning communities" (PLCs).

Dufour, Dufour, Eaker, and Many (2006) are the best representatives of this good work. They bring together six core components of PLCs: a focus on learning, a collaborative culture, collective inquiry, an action orientation, a commitment to continuous learning, and a concentration on results. The problem is that the term *PLC* travels faster than the concept. PLCs are not the latest innovation, but they are often treated that way. Rather, they are intended to permanently change the culture of the school toward continuous improvement.

Changing cultures is the principal's hardest job because there is so much previous structure and culture to overcome. This is turning out to be even harder than expected. It is about professional learning, not professional development. As Elmore (2000) observes:

> The job of administrative leaders is primarily about enhancing the skills and knowledge of people in the organization, creating a common culture of expectations around the use of those skills and knowledge, holding the various pieces of the organization together in a producing relationship with each other, and holding individuals accountable for their contributions to the collective result (p. 15)

Elmore (2004) sharpens this point when he says "improvement is . . . a function of learning to do the right things *in the setting where you work*" (p. 73, emphasis added). But—and this is the central issue:

> The problem [is that] there is almost no opportunity for teachers
> to engage in continuous and sustained learning about their prac-
> tice . . . observing and being observed by their colleagues in their
> own classrooms and classrooms of other teachers in other schools
> confronting similar problems. (p. 127)

This is indeed the nub of the problem, and not many businesses get it right. When these few companies do focus on culture, their productivity soars. Sisodia, Wolfe, and Sheth in *Firms of Endearment* (2007), identify 28 companies by name (Starbucks, Whole Foods, etc.) who met "humanistic performance" criteria (for example, they paid equal attention to employees and customers). Matching these companies with Jim Collins's (2001) 11 "Great Companies," Siso-dia and colleagues discovered that their companies outperformed Collins's set, over a 10-year period, by 1,026% financial gain to 331%—a 3 to 1 ratio.

So the heart of what's worth fighting for within the school is creating deep cultures that work daily on purposeful, continuous learning. This has the short-term effect of improving learning, but it also establishes legacy conditions. All leaders eventually leave, but it is not turnover of leaders, per se, that is the issue; what matters is *continuity of good direction*. Principals who establish collaborative cultures increase the likelihood that there will be this continuity of direction because it is already built into the culture, and culture has powerful persistence. Culture *is* legacy.

LINKING TO THE OUTSIDE

Tending to the internal culture is not enough. Principals who cultivate stand-alone collaborative schools undercut the chances for continuity because system context is always more powerful than that of a single school.

There are two main reasons why we advocate schools learning from one another, or what we call "lateral capacity building." The first is that district-wide reform depends on schools leveraging one another forward. When school leaders commit to giving and receiving ideas, knowledge of best practice flows and identity with peers and the larger system is enhanced. The second is that the give-and-take with other schools is a source of pressure and support for one's own internal development.

If individual schools are not part of the bigger picture, it is unlikely that leadership succession will amount to anything but "unplanned discontinuity," as Hargreaves and Fink (2006) found in the majority of their cases. Successful planned continuity is a scarce commodity in school leadership: "Succession plans either go awry, or there is no real planning at all" (p. 71). Individual principals help the continuity of their schools by integrating themselves and their staff into the horizontal and vertical culture of the district.

LEAVING FOND MEMORIES

Happiness and leaving behind fond memories are closely related. John Haidt (2006) carefully unpacked *The Happiness Hypothesis*. He concludes that happiness is neither inside nor outside ourselves, but rather "comes from between" (p. 213). Happiness is relational—who we are in relation to people and to our environment.

Paraphrasing Haidt, happiness is derived from a combination of four elements: love (having meaningful attachments in life), meaningful work, vital engagement, and what he calls cross-level coherence (when your sense of purpose of contribution meshes with the larger culture of which you are a part).

Paradoxically, leaders are more likely to secure some immortality by not trying to ensure it. Hargreaves and Fink observe that leaders often like the limelight and are reluctant to face the facts of succession, and that many want to signal their immortality by building great monuments or by naming their successor. This is one way to be remembered, but not necessarily fondly.

Happiness as defined by Haidt fits perfectly with legacy. These qualities enable leaders to make an immediate and lasting contribution. If too much depends on the power of the individual leader—no matter how great he or she is—then there is little to carry that influence forward. Dominance today leads to dissipation tomorrow.

All and all, paying attention to legacy from Day 1 is good for both the present and the future. Leave your legacy today and tomorrow will take care of itself.

CHAPTER 3

Leading
Knowledgeably

In our book *Breakthrough*, Peter Hill, Carmel Crévola, and I argued that the last frontier of instructional improvement is getting behind the classroom door (Fullan, Hill, & Crévola, 2006). De-privatizing teaching involves opening up the world of the classroom to scrutiny and continuous development of instruction.

The recent McKinsey and Company report on the world's best-performing school systems essentially drew the same conclusions:

> The top performing school systems recognized that the only way to improve outcomes is to improve instruction; learning occurs when students and teachers interact, and thus improving learning implies improving the quality of that instruction. They understood which interventions were effective to improve instruction—coaching, practical teacher training, developing stronger school leaders, and enabling teachers to learn from each other—and then found ways to deliver those interventions across their school systems. (Barber & Mourshed, 2007, p. 26)

OPENING THE "'BLACK BOX" OF INSTRUCTION

This is the domain of the principal leading knowledgeably, which is to say opening the "black box" of instruction and helping the school sort out what needs to be known—about the child, about teaching and learning, and about the use of data as a strategy for both improvement and accountability. We laid out the key messages in *Breakthrough*:

1. To make a substantial difference in outcomes, the next phase of reform must focus on what has typically been the "black box" in education reform—classroom instruction.
2. The focus must be on improving classroom instruction and adopting processes for turning it into a more precise, validated, data-driven, expert activity that can respond to the learning needs of individual students.
3. This requires diagnostic practitioners who have a solid core of beliefs and understandings, a deep moral purpose, and the ability to develop highly personalized classroom programs.
4. It requires systems that will support the day-to-day transformation of instruction for all students at all levels, including the classroom, the school, the district, and the state.
5. These systems will bring expert knowledge to bear on the detailed daily instructional decisions that teachers make. Maps of the pathways and detours followed by students in learning a defined area of the curriculum will be constructed and built into "critical learning instructional paths" (CLIP) that provide a framework for guiding instruction and monitoring learning.

There is a ton of knowledge compressed in those five statements, and the principal must free him- or herself from the vise-like grip of constraints discussed in Chapter 1. Leading knowledgeably must be the core role of the principal.

We also make the fundamental point that solving the need for pinpointed instruction must be done not through teacher-proof *prescriptive* methods, but rather through the never-ending process of continually refining *precision* of teaching as fit for the needs of a particular child on a particular day.

Further, we argued that this will not work if we try to do it on the backs of already overloaded teachers. This is where the principal comes in—by knowing how to achieve precision in a way that makes the teacher's task easier, and definitely more effective and more rewarding. The more we have school principals who can lead knowledgeably, the more feasible this goal becomes.

PURSUING THE PRECISION QUEST

Recently, some excellent resources have become available to enable instructional leaders to pursue the precision quest. In addition to our own CLIP model in *Breakthrough*, Marzano's *The Art and Science of Teaching* (2007) furnishes "a comprehensive framework for instruction." There is also Black and colleagues' (2003) wonderful set of strategies for developing "assessment for learning" and engaging students in the role of evaluation and learning as teaching techniques are altered. All of this is of vital importance. Quoting Nye and colleagues (2004), Marzano reports:

> Students who have a teacher at the 75th percentile in terms of pedagogical competence will outgain students who have a teacher at the 25th percentile by 14 percentile points in reading and 18 percentile in mathematics . . . students who have a 90th percentile teacher will outgain students who have a 50th percentile teacher by 13 percentile points in reading and 18 percentile points in mathematics. (p. 2)

Leading knowledgeably means bringing all teachers to a high level of pedagogical effectiveness; but more than that, it means fostering interactions that keep teachers at that level through continuous application and refinement. This is not to be taken lightly—millions of dollars have already been spent on standards, curriculum, assessment, and professional development, only to find that the intervention is not strong enough to have an impact in the classroom. The reason that principals are so important is that they are on the scene. If anyone can influence teachers on a day-to-day basis, it is the principal, both directly and indirectly through the teacher leaders he or she selects.

The McKinsey study stresses that focusing on instruction by itself is not enough. You also need to find ways to actually change what happens within the classroom. Three things in particular have to happen:

- Individual teachers need to become aware of the specific weaknesses in their own practice. In most cases, this involves teachers becoming aware of both their own practice and of the underlying mind-sets that were driving it.
- Individual teachers must gain a precise knowledge of better practice. Generally, this can only be achieved through a demonstration of proven best practice in an authentic setting.
- Individual teachers must be motivated to make the improvement. This *cannot* be achieved by changing material incentives, but instead requires a deeper change in motivation. Teams of teachers feeling high expectations all share a sense of purpose and, above all, a collective belief in their common ability to make a difference for the children they serve (Barber & Mourshed, 2007).

In addition to de-privatizing instruction, there needs to be an explicit and transparent commitment to linking teaching *practices* to student-learning *outcomes*. Certain practices under certain conditions do lead to certain results. Therefore, principals and teachers need to assure themselves that one thing is truly leading to another. Causal connections in complex situations are not straightforward, so there needs to be a lot of discussion and examination of plausible linkages between actions and outcomes.

LINKING THE RESULTS

Transparency of results over time must also become standard practice. We have already done this with literacy and numeracy.

As stated in Chapter 1, schools need to do these comparisons in this order of importance:

> First, they need to compare themselves with themselves (referencing their own starting points). How are we doing in literacy and math now, compared to last year and the year before? (We recommend 3-year windows to determine movement up or down or stagnation.)
> Second, they need to compare their performance with other schools facing similar circumstances—the so-called apples-with-apples consideration. This is fair and reasonable, and can usually tell you if you have something to learn, or something valuable to share.
> Third, schools must keep in mind how they are doing relative to some external standard, such as 100% success or the average success of the province, the state, or the country as a whole.

We have found that, once schools get involved in instructional improvement as it links to results, they become more at ease with assessment data. Indeed, they eagerly look forward to external assessments to see how they are doing. As a bonus, they become much more comfortable with explaining themselves to the community or to the hierarchy. They literally are more competent and more confident about what is going on, and in identifying what the underlying explanations might be.

DEVELOPING A CULTURE OF IMPROVEMENT

Precision of practice and transparency of both practice and its connection to results is extremely difficult to build into ongoing cultures. But this is the mark of effective organizations in all sectors—that these cultures are very much in the minority attests to how much diligence is required on the part of organizational leaders to establish and maintain such cultures. One of my *Six Secrets of Change* is that learning *is* the work (Fullan, 2008). This means that learning to improve things must be built into the day-to-day culture of the work. Learning cannot be left to external workshops or courses. This secret is essentially about precision and learning. The following stories present some of the parallels I found in other sectors.

Atul Gawande is a general surgeon at the Brigham and Women's Hospital in Boston. His most recent book, *Better* (2007), is a great concrete example of how effective organizations need to diligently and consistently apply what they know, while still seeking to get "better" at what they do.

Let's start with a seemingly straightforward test: doctors and nurses regularly washing their hands. Gawande reports that every year, 2 million Americans acquire an infection while they are in a hospital, and that 90,000 of these people die of the infection. At the same time, the greatest difficulty hospital administrators have "is getting clinicians like me to do the one thing that consistently halts the spread of infections: wash your hands" (p. 14). Hospital statistics show that "we doctors and nurses wash our hands one-third to one-half as often as we are supposed to" (p. 15). Precision involves the pursuit of perfection. Even when compliance rates for proper hand hygiene were improved from 40% to 70% in Gawande's hospital, infection rates did not decline—because the 30% who did not wash their hands still left plenty of opportunities to transmit infections.

Successful organizations mobilize themselves to be *all over given practices that are known to make a difference*. In Gawande's hospital, anything short of an "obsession with hand washing has begun to seem inadequate" (p. 20). It took constant education, convenience of hand washing facilities, and frequent random spot checks to monitor and improve the performance of something as simple as washing one's hands regularly.

Gawande says it is all about cultivating habits of "diligence," "doing it right," and "ingenuity." It is not waiting for the answer from research (although it does entail continually seeking test knowledge): "In the absence of certainty, the truth is that we want doctors who fight. . . . Always fight. Always look for what more you could do" (pp. 159, 161).

We see time and again that having new technology is not the cure. What is the cure is what Gawande calls "the infant science of improving performance" (p. 242). Gawande might as well have been writing about Toyota.

LEARNING DURING PERFORMANCE

Toyota has made a science out of improving performance. Liker and Meier (2007) spell it out chapter and verse. The essence of Toyota's approach to improving performance in any and all areas consists of three components:

1. Identify critical knowledge.
2. Transfer knowledge using job instruction.
3. Verify learning and success.

As Liker and Meier observe, "this is not a 'project,' but rather a 'process' [that] will require continued and sustained effort *forever*" (p. 82, emphasis in original).

Liker and Meier make a crucial point about relentless consistency: that going about identifying and standardizing critical knowledge is not just for technical tasks like the assembly line, but applies to *all* jobs. To illustrate this they use three examples: manufacturing (bumper molding operator), a nurse in a busy hospital, and an entry-level design engineer. This universal applicability is a key message: Consistency and innovation can and must go together, and you achieve them by applying organized learning in context.

I won't go into the technical details of the three examples examined by Liker and Meier, but we do need to appreciate what is going on in those cases. They state: "we estimate that Toyota spends five times as much time detailing work methods and developing talent in employees as any other company we have seen" (p. 110). And "if we are to identify the single greatest difference between Toyota and other organizations (this includes service, health care, and manufacturing organizations), it would be *the depth of understanding* among Toyota employees regarding their work" (p. 112, emphasis added).

On the question of whether focusing on consistency of practice inhibits creativity, Liker and Meier respond that Toyota is producing "intentional mindfulness," rather than "mindless conforming." Toyota, they observe, places a very high value on creativity, thinking ability, and problem solving. None of this is static: During performance, there is constant learning about whether this is detecting and correcting common errors, or discovering new ways to improve.

So, it is essential for school leaders to foster relentless consistency relative to those practices that are known to be effective— practices that come to have the status of being "non-negotiable." We need more assertive principals in this regard. At the same time, creativity and problem-solving must be valued in the culture. Consistency of effective practice and continuous improvement are decidedly *not* mutually exclusive.

The best of research confirms just how crucial instructional leadership is for improving student learning. Viviane Robinson and her colleagues at The University of Auckland, New Zealand, conducted a thorough worldwide examination of the research evidence on the relationship between school leadership and student outcomes (Robinson, 2007; Robinson, Hohepa, & Lloyd, 2007).

Using a high standard methodology of "best evidence synthesis," Robinson and her colleagues found that the popular "transformational leadership" of "inspiring staff through a vision which energizes and encourages them to work collaboratively towards a common goal" (p. 39) was three times less impactful on student learning outcomes than "instructional or pedagogical leadership" that entails "close involvement of leadership in establishing the academic mission and a school culture and routines which are supportive of that mission" (p. 42). It is the specific, targeted actions that count.

In closer examination, the "effect sizes" of principals promoting and participating directly with teachers in the formal and informal learning of the use of data to influence appropriate instructional activities was more than twice as powerful as any other leadership dimension. Once again, we see precise knowledge being mobilized to make a difference of the kind we have documented in *Breakthrough* (Fullan, Hill, & Crévola, 2006), and in *The Six Secrets of Change* (Fullan, 2008).

It is important to note that Robinson and colleagues are reporting on "research findings." As always, *WWFFP* is about the harder work of "action." Doing is much more than knowing. The spirit of the guidelines for action in Chapter 6 integrate "knowing and doing"—the essence of What's Worth Fighting For.

In short, leading knowledgeably is at the core of all highly effective organizations. It is worth fighting for because it is extremely hard to achieve (and thus requires a fighter), and yet is essential. Knowledge is literally the substance of change. It represents the means of all accomplishments. Principals, as leaders closest to the scene, do not leave it to others to ensure that knowledge is front-and-center in the work of the school.

CHAPTER 4

Leading
Learning
Communities

We have already covered some of the territory on leading learning communities in our legacy discussion of collaborative cultures (Chapter 2) and in our treatment of teaching knowledgeably (Chapter 3). But let's sharpen the point with more examples of what it looks like in practice.

The research knowledge on leading learning communities has been around for a while. What's worth fighting for involves putting it into practice.

THE KNOWLEDGE BASE

Over a quarter-century ago, Judith Little (1981) made the best case for how teachers and principals should work together to accomplish meaningful reform:

> School improvement is most surely and thoroughly achieved when: Teachers engage in frequent, continuous and increasingly concrete and precise *talk* about teaching practice (as distinct from [talk] about the foibles and failures of students and their families, and the unfortunate demands of society on the school). By such talk, teachers build up a shared language adequate to the complexity of teaching, capable of distinguishing one practice and its virtue from another.

Teachers and administrators frequently *observe* each other teaching and provide each other with useful (if potentially frightening) evaluations of their teaching. Only such observation and feedback . . . provide the precision and concreteness, which make the talk about teaching useful. (pp. 12–13, emphasis in original)

Fifteen years later, Kruse, Louis, and Bryk (1995) succinctly made a similar case from their research on professional learning communities. They note that five critical elements undergird effective PLCs: reflective dialogue, de-privatization of practice, collective focus on student learning, collaboration, and shared norms and values. Then they identify two sets of necessary conditions. One set is "structural"—in particular, time to meet and talk, interdependent teaching roles, and communication structures. A second needed set of conditions is referred to as "social and human resources" (what we would call "culture"), and includes openness to improvement, trust and respect, skill base, supportive leadership, and socialization of new and current staff.

Earlier, Susan Rosenholtz (1989) had drawn on the importance of community in documenting the difference between "stuck" and "moving" schools, which she alternatively labeled as "learning impoverished" and "learning enriched" schools. She contrasts the two sets of schools. Stuck schools are characterized by:

Little attachment to anything or anybody. Teachers seemed more concerned with their own identity than a sense of shared community. Teachers learned about the nature of their work randomly, not deliberately, tending to follow their individual instincts. Without shared governance, particularly in managing student conduct, the absolute number of students who claimed teachers' attention seemed greater. . . . Teachers talked of frustration, failure, tedium and managed to transfer those attributes to the students about whom they complained. (p. 208)

By contrast, in "moving" schools, Rosenholtz found that,

Where teachers request from and offer technical assistance to each other, and where school staff enforced consistent standards for student behavior, teachers tend to complain less about students and parents. Further, where teachers collaborate, where they keep parents involved and informed about their children's progress, where teachers and principals work together to consistently enforce standards for student behavior, and where teachers celebrate their achievements through positive feedback from students, parents, principals, colleagues and their own sense, they collectively tend to believe in a technical culture and their instructional practice. (p. 137)

The above research findings have been consistent over several decades, but little action has followed to put the findings into practice. Kruse and colleagues made the following recommendation in 1995: "Professional community within schools has been a minor theme in many education reform efforts since the 1960s. Perhaps it is time that it became a major rallying cry among reformers, rather than a secondary whisper" (p. 6). Since the 1960s! Knowledge that was largely ignored for 4 decades is now being taken seriously, albeit with the caveat that many of the new efforts are relatively superficial. But at least the game is on.

THE ACTION BASE

We have been working for the past 5 years with the York Region District School Board just outside Toronto. York Region is a large, growing, multicultural district with 151 elementary schools and 30 high schools. With many recent immigrants whose first language is one other than English, more than 100 different languages are spoken in the schools.

York Region has made priorities of literacy and numeracy, and uses collaborative cultures within and across schools as the main means to get there. In fact, the strategy is called "The Literacy Collaborative."

Virtually all schools have moved forward, and we have written in detail about York Region's district-wide reform efforts (Fullan, 2007; Sharratt & Fullan, 2006). Here I take two schools—one elementary and one secondary—as specific examples.

Looking at Effective Collaboration: Two Examples

Jersey Public School is a large multicultural elementary school. Its scores in reading, writing, and math—as assessed annually by an independent provincial agency, the Education Quality and Accountability Office—were languishing well below 50% in 2001–2002, prior to the collaborative reform effort. In particular, the school focused on improving students' writing starting with two basic questions:

> Why are our struggling writers stalled?
>
> How could we change our teaching practice to more effectively address the needs of struggling writers? (All quotes are taken from Jersey Public School, 2007.)

You will notice that the collaborative schools I am talking about pursue improvement with increasing precision and focus. They are literally all over the problem. Jersey proceeded to investigate these questions:

> How can we improve student achievement in writing by increasing student engagement?
>
> What does student engagement look and sound like? How can we design, model and share writing lessons that build and sustain student engagement?
>
> How can we support the growth of deeper in-class collaboration at Jersey?

Led by the principal and a school leadership team, they became more specific by identifying and looking for what they called "Road Signs":

> Deeper understanding of the importance of explicit academic and social goals.
>
> Clearer understanding of how our students respond positively when writing for an authentic purpose and real audience.

Continued emphasis on ways to provide targeted, effective feedback during the writing process.

As they proceeded, they tackled the harder question of "how to create the time, will and trust to help us grow this process within our school culture." The staff knew their research literature, citing Richard Elmore (2004): Successful professional development is likely to occur in schools and classroom settings, rather than off site, and it is likely to involve work with individual teachers or small groups around the observation of actual teaching.

Does this attention to detail work? Consider the grade-3 reading, writing, and math scores shown in Table 4.1.

TABLE 4.1. Literacy Scores for Jersey Public
(percentage of grade-3 students achieving proficiency on the provincial tests)

	Reading	Writing	Math
2001–2002	36	36	51
2005–2006	60	60	80

How about high schools, which many think are impervious to collaborative cultures? Thornhill Secondary School in York Region is a typical large high school with great ethnic diversity. Let's take the problem of how to achieve 100% literacy for high school students. Ontario has a mandatory grade-10 (age 16 or so) literacy test called the Ontario Secondary School Literacy Test (OSSLT). Students are required to pass this test in order to graduate from high school, but they can take the test again if they fail on their first attempt.

Thornhill, like all 181 schools in the district, presents its accomplishments for the year at a Learning Fair held each June to celebrate success and spur further development. When you get into the details of Thornhill's presentation, you see relentless precision in action. In 2006, 88% of students taking the grade-10 literacy test were successful. The school knows by name and profile the 41 students who did not pass (27 males and 14 females; 24 English as a second language, etc.). Of students who were "previously eligible" and were taking the test either for the second time or had had a deferral, similar details are known (11 of the 16 ESL students were unsuccessful, etc.).

Then we see the solutions at work. There are five overlapping interventions:

- After-school literacy programs for ESL students
- Workshops for small groups of grade-11/12 students who have not yet met the requirement
- A literacy blitz for grade-10 students led by all teachers in the school, whatever their subject
- A hugely successful PLANT (Peer Literacy and Numeracy Team) program, where selected students in grades 11 and 12 are trained and supported to work individually with struggling students who have not yet passed the OSSLT (PLANT has just been extended to science)
- A Guided Literacy Strategy where teachers do individual tutoring

Every program is continually evaluated and refined. For example, surveys ask teachers and students how well the literacy blitz worked from their experience, and how it could be improved. Every individual student who misses a session is contacted by the literacy teachers or school administrator, not to be chastised but to figure out how to increase participation. Students are surveyed to determine whether they were comfortable in attending sessions, and are not made to feel stigmatized (the vast majority liked and appreciated the sessions).

Thornhill also compared its performance against the district's average as a whole (30 schools), and against the province's average, striving to better itself at each stage. Students are asked details: Do you have a better understanding of each of the four segments of the OSSLT test—(1) reading and multiple choice; (2) short writing tasks and newspaper articles; (3) reading and short answers; and (4) writing multiple choice and expression? With respect to the PLANT program, the school surveys students concerning the extent to which there is rapport between tutors and tutees "that is risk-free" and an environment where it is "safe to learn."

There is nothing fancy about Jersey's and Thornhill's improvement strategies. They are simply and powerfully systematic and thorough. Most of all, none of the ideas, results, and analysis are presented by the likes of Little, Kruse, Rosenholtz, or Fullan. It is the principal and the teachers who describe with pride and precision the theories of action under way, how far they have proceeded and why, and what the next steps are. When this happens, you know that professional learning communities are being led—on the ground, where it counts.

Rearranging the Principal's Role to Develop Collaboration

The key to leading learning communities is for the principal to position him- or herself to do three main things:

1. Elevate instruction as the mainstay of the role.
2. Explicitly figure out how to delegate managerial tasks to others—plant, finance, personnel, health and safety, and bureaucratic demands.
3. Ensure that the instructional work is carried out through distributive leadership (a much misunderstood concept).

Let's look at each of these priorities.

First, principals must make teaching and learning the driving focus. There is a choice here. We saw from the PriceWaterhouseCoopers study (2007) that some principals spend their time on managerial tasks (the system can make this problem worse), while others, a minority, make teaching and learning the reigning priority. There are several critical elements:

1. Select a small number of ambitious instructional goals. In elementary schools, this means literacy and numeracy and their positive side effects. In secondary schools, it includes literacy, but fundamentally means personal connection with individual students, engaging them in learning options that fit or stimulate their needs.

2. Work intensely on instruction—the black box of teaching and learning practices within each and every classroom.

3. Establish daily "assessment for learning" methods, which all teachers can use to link the individual learning needs of a student to the appropriate instructional response.

4. Embed the norm that all teachers have an obligation to contribute to the learning of other teachers in the school, and to learn from the other teachers.

5. Extend the learning norm to encompass contributing to and learning from sources outside the school—such as other local schools and the profession at large.

6. Devote and align all major elements (budget, professional learning, meetings, communication inside and outside of the school) to the cause of the previous five elements.

Second, a large part of being successful with the instructional core consists of figuring out how to handle the growing managerial demands that, if mishandled, become dominant distractions to the main agenda. The first way to do this is not to count on "the system" to get it right. We will get to the system in a moment, but a large part of the problem is self-imposed: Principals have not kept up with or cultivated their instructional expertise. Of course, principals who become out-of-touch with instructional issues gravitate toward the more concrete, tangible operational tasks.

I am saying that principals should make ongoing instructional expertise a priority for themselves, as well as for their teachers.

They should model the priorities they espouse. "What's worth fighting for" is about individual action. So the message is that making instruction the core preoccupation is first an individual responsibility—that is to say, the principal must fight for this, regardless of what the system does.

The system actually can help a lot. All the things that I have said about school culture apply in spades to the district. District-wide cultures that prioritize instruction act accordingly in allocation of budget resources for professional learning, and capacity-building activities for schools. They are, in turn, responsive to and supportive of principals who act on the instructional agenda, and impatient with school principals who remain in the managerial mode.

The principal who is focused on leading a learning community has to figure out how to run an effective school without actually doing the managerial and operational work. Many bureaucratic requirements can be handled by top-notch administrative staff. Others on the leadership team can take specific responsibilities—for example, discipline and behavior codes.

A strong step forward (and a system responsibility) is to create and train people for a new role as business manager. England has done just that with its National College for School Leadership, providing certificates and diplomas in school business management. External research recently documented that business managers in high schools save $15 per pupil and raise $100 per pupil, and that, on average, school business managers in primary schools save $30 and raise $120 per student (Munby, 2007). In smaller districts, one business manager can serve three or four schools. There may be other alternatives to the business manager solution (such as providing additional resources and training for assistant principals in this role), but, whatever the case, action is badly needed to address the managerial tasks at the school level.

Principals can already delegate more than most do. And in the future, systems could rarely make a wiser decision than to create, train, and certify school business managers to handle all human resources, finance, site management, and health and safety matters—a strong recommendation I make in Chapter 6.

The third way principals can create learning communities is through distributive leadership, but this term is so vague, I suggest that we drop it. "Growing tomorrow's leaders today" is a better way of putting it. Leadership is not distributed, it is interactively shared—thereby coalescing the collective effort of the staff. It is about modeling effective leadership for others and cultivating leadership development in others for the double payoff of greater immediate impact and the establishment of a pipeline of future leaders.

Steve Munby, the CEO of the NCSL in England, sees helping teachers develop other teachers as one of the college's top priorities. He cites numerous examples of school heads taking talent development seriously by "molding good leadership by coaching, praising and empowering others" (Munby, 2007, p. 7). At a secondary school in Islington (part of greater London), for example, there are 18 members of the staff who want to become principals and attend weekly leadership development sessions that the school runs for them: "The enthusiasm about leadership is palpable and is modeled by the enthusiasm and commitment of the head teacher who has introduced the program into the school" (p. 8). Imagine the pipeline for future school leaders if many schools engaged in this practice of explicitly preparing such leaders.

In sum, principals who simultaneously elevate instruction, delegate managerial tasks to others, and go about their work by growing tomorrow's leaders today, end up creating lasting learning communities.

In the last three chapters, I have said that school leaders need to lead legacies, knowledge systems, and learning communities. These three components are intertwined. But there is one more reality they must not neglect: namely, the system as a whole. System is context, and context is never neutral. It can help or hinder in powerful ways. System context is too important to leave to system leaders.

CHAPTER 5

Leading Systems

The perennial problem facing large-scale education systems is how to achieve a degree of cohesion. Nothing seems to work. Tighten the ship with clear moral goals, standards, and accountability at the top, and the system barely moves. Swing to site-based empowerment and you get a combination of pockets of (unsustainable) success, along with some nonresponsive schools and some schools going backward.

Believe it or not, the school principal has a responsibility to help with *system cohesion*, and in many ways is in the best position from which to make a contribution. They can do this in three ways:

1. Through links to other schools
2. Through building relationships with district leaders
3. Through connecting to the goals of the system as a whole

PURPOSEFUL PEER INTERACTION

One of my six "secrets of change" that applies to all organizations, regardless of sector, is called "connect peers with purpose" (Fullan, 2008, Ch. 2). In human systems, the glue that holds things together is always *social*. What you need in large systems is to figure out how to capture focus in a diverse world. Since top-down and bottom-up doesn't solve this problem, the answer has to lie in finessing simultaneous tight–loose systems.

Tight–loose systems do have direction: Leaders at the top have to set goals (interactively), establish monitoring, invest in capacity-building, and so on. The secret is that cohesion and focus are best achieved more through fostering purposeful peer interaction among principals than they are directly through the hierarchy.

There are many reasons why principals should seek peer interaction with other schools. We saw one of them earlier. If a principal runs an isolated school, no matter how collaborative and successful it is in its own right, it will inevitably be vulnerable any time there is succession of leadership. I have also made the case that, if you are in a system where other principals are working on collaborative cultures, not only do you have something to learn, but you can also take advantage of the right kind of pressure—peer pressure—as you and your staff see what others are doing, especially if they are, perhaps, accomplishing more than you.

And then again, if you are sharing with others what you are learning, you are contributing to the development of other schools around you. This is not as altruistic as it seems (although there is nothing wrong with that) because if other schools get better, the context improves, and that can only help you. After all, who is family here? Other schools in the system.

The conditions for peer interaction across schools have dramatically improved over the past 5 or so years, as Thomas Friedman makes crystal clear in *The World Is Flat* (2005). Friedman identifies a triple convergence. The first is technology, the global web that "enabled multiple forms of collaboration—sharing of knowledge and work—in real time, without regard to geographic distance" (p. 126). The second convergence involved new ways of doing business, in which managers take advantage of the new, flatter playing field to develop "horizontal collaboration and value-orientation processes and habits" (p. 178). The third convergence comes from the expansion of participation of those billions of people who were previously excluded from the playing field—people in China, India, Russia, Eastern Europe, Latin America, and Asia.

Whether you go far afield or stay in the neighborhood, interacting with other schools is a good idea. And because it seems inevitable, you might as well get good at it. We saw in Chapter

1 that substantial benefits accrued to at least 75% of the 300 high schools participating in the RATL project in England (Hargreaves & Shirley, 2006). Brian Caldwell furnishes countless examples of schools working purposefully in clusters, especially in England and Australia. To take just one of the numerous examples described by Caldwell (2006), consider a cluster of six elementary schools in rural Australia that focus on literacy and numeracy, facilitated by a cluster deputy principal:

1. All staff in each of the six schools meet together in the sixth week of each term to consider matters of priority as identified in the plan for the year.
2. A cluster deputy principal was appointed in 2004. The appointee is recognized as a deputy principal of each of these schools . . . the primary role is capacity-building across the cluster.
3. An executive teacher specializing in mathematics is based at Lanyon High and provides services to each school with sharing of costs.
4. Technical support in ICT is also shared across schools.
5. An integrated curriculum designed at Charles Conder Primary was readily shared among all primary schools in the cluster.
6. A number of primary teachers "followed" their year 6 students to Lanyon High as part of a transition strategy. (pp. 98–99)

No matter how you cut it, school principals have new opportunities and new obligations to help their schools participate in purposeful peer networks. The school benefits, the system benefits.

RELATIONSHIPS WITHIN THE DISTRICT

We have already strayed into this territory in the previous section. This is not a book about *the role of* the district, but about how principals *relate to* the district. If principals are fortunate enough to be in a district that uses peer networks as a strategy, this provides the opportunity to embrace learning from other schools. Again we have many concrete examples. Indeed, *WWFFP*'s ideas are all drawn from actual real-life examples.

Let's return to York Region, a highly multicultural district with 120,000 students. York district's central leadership and its more than 300 principals and vice principals in 151 elementary and 30 secondary schools have been working on a collaborative culture agenda for 8 years. Their core strategy is called "The Literacy Collaborative." The key features of their strategy are:

- A clearly articulated vision and commitment to literacy for all students, which is continually the subject of communication in the district
- A system-wide comprehensive plan and framework for continuous improvement
- Using data to inform instruction and determine resources
- Building administrator and teacher capacity to teach literacy to all students
- Establishing professional learning communities at all levels of the system and beyond the district

All 181 schools participate through school leadership teams (always led by the principal) in cohorts of schools focused on improving instructional practice in the classroom as it "causally" links to increased student achievement. It works. Student achievement across the district, after being flat-lined, has gone up some 10% in the last 5 years. Morale of teachers and principals is higher. On a survey asking whether "teachers share expertise and effective practices with teachers from other schools," 69% reported that it was occurring with a substantial impact (responding with a 4 or 5 on five-point scale). Remember, this is a very big district.

Another good example involves Boston Public Schools. Their plan is based on six essentials:

- Effective instruction as the core essential
- A focus on student work and data

- Professional learning on the part of teachers and principals
- Shared leadership
- Additional and focused resources
- Families and community involvement

All these ideas are familiar to us from *WWFFP*.

Literacy and numeracy test scores in Boston have increased steadily since 1999 for all race and ethnic groups (Black, White, Asian, and Hispanic), with some essential leveling off (what we call the *plateau effect*—a temporary condition of consolidation). McLaughlin and Talbert (2006) summarize the positive impact in these words:

> Multiple evaluations show that Boston's approach to instruction [and] to collaborative coaching and learning are benefiting students and teachers. Student outcomes have improved, as have relationships between teachers and students and among teachers. Boston sees other positive system-level consequences of their strategy—enhanced coherence, increased accountability at all levels, and increased buy-in from district educators. (pp. 126–127)

The last few paragraphs have been from the district's perspective, so to speak. *WWFFP* is primarily (but not exclusively) about the principal's perspective. Two implications stand out. First, principals should participate in horizontal interaction with peers. As we have seen, this helps principals at the same time that it helps other schools. Second, principals should think of the district as a resource. Ideally, principals should contribute to and experience a strong two-way relationship with district leadership in terms of communication and mutual influence. We have seen this clearly and beneficially in York Region, in Boston, and in many other situations.

Even if the district does not have its act together in this respect, it is important for principals to try to move this agenda forward. We have worked with some districts in which it was the principals as a group that, in the early stages, pushed for more emphasis on collaboration, professional learning communities, and a district

focus on strategies for continuous instructional improvement. Most often, district leaders responded positively, and most often, a change in the superintendency reinforced the new developments. After all, what superintendent would not welcome school principals who are willing to put energy into instruction—not only in their own school, but in relation to other schools? School and district reform is decidedly a "we–we" proposition.

TOTAL SYSTEM CONNECTION

The *total system* is the state, province, or country. One might say that the government level is too removed from the world of the principal, but this need not, and should not, be the case. System context is too important to leave it to politicians. Heifetz and Linsky (2002) capture the main idea with a metaphor. Leaders these days, they say, must be able to be both in the balcony and on the dance floor, moving iteratively back and forth. They must drill down in achieving precision and continuous improvement, but they must also be aware of and connect to the bigger picture.

This is the simultaneous tight–loose solution. Principals should not think that their role is to implement somebody else's agenda (in this case, the government's), but they should be aware of the bigger picture. They should look for points of connection. The government should not be the enemy. The more common agendas that can be found, the better.

In Ontario for the past 4 years, the government has been vigorously pursuing a literacy and numeracy agenda. It has invited local districts and schools to help shape implementation (but not to determine whether they should be priorities). What elementary school principal would not have literacy as a priority? For that matter, what high school principal would not work on improving literacy (recall our Thornhill Secondary School example)? What's worth fighting for is to have core instructional priorities coincide for both schools and governments. Principals should not see the government as only "political." The connections do not have to be many,

but the school and the system are better off if they can identify key common priorities and jointly pursue them. In October 2007, the government was reelected for another 4 years, with a resounding mandate from the electorate to continue and deepen improvements in the public school system.

This is not a pipe dream. The National College of School Leadership in England boldly embraces the theme "School leaders as system leaders" (www.ncsl.org.uk). Partly, this is attitudinal. The advice is to know, take into account, and link to government policies in education reform. It is also concrete. There are now many examples of "executive heads" who run more than one school, and of districts and governments who fund partnerships of schools with higher and lower performance.

England has now gone so far as to establish a National Leaders of Education initiative, in which the National College carefully identifies and cultivates high-performing school heads who are interested in making a contribution beyond their school—by mentoring other school leaders in struggling schools, or by participating in structured critical policy discussions with ministers of education on current and possible future stages of reform.

Let's be clear. I am not advocating that principals devote themselves to the larger system at the expense of their schools. We need to be cautious here because principals are already overloaded. Two things are practical, however. One is that the principal is well advised to be aware of and to try to connect with system-level goals and strategies. If this is done in conjunction with the district, all the better. The second, as we saw with the NCSL, is that there should be more opportunities for principals to leave their school to play a so-called "system role."

If we return to our "growing leaders of the future theme," what could be more powerful than having some of the best incumbent principals help in developing other current or would-be school leaders? Remember—and this is absolutely critical—that this is not the principal as *savior*; it is the principal developing other teachers to be self-sufficient. These teachers can, in turn, model this approach in developing still others—a multiplier effect that improves the whole system, now and for the future. Finally, let us emphasize again that we are not working on system solutions in this book from the point of system leaders. I am recommending that principals *themselves* show an interest in the contexts that surround them and affect them, for better or for worse.

The reason that this chapter is important concerns the fact that cohesion and coherence remain a most elusive quality in large, complex systems. The problem cannot be solved by direct command and control strategies—there are too many moving pieces that have minds of their own. This chapter suggests, instead, that there are more effective indirect methods.

Stimulating purposeful interaction—horizontally and vertically—provides the glue that helps complex systems to focus. Leaders at the top cannot achieve coherence in the system because there are just too few of them. But if peers are employed in the service of coherence, there are enough forces at work to do the job.

Interaction of the kind I have been advocating across these chapters sorts out differences as you go. And because evidence-informed decisionmaking is built-in, weak practices are jettisoned and more effective ones are retained. Because it is a social process, what gets retained is by definition *shared*—both in terms of meaning and of competence. It is best to try to avoid the extremes of isolation (where no one influences anyone) and group-think (where the group squelches individualism).

Of course, what I described in the previous paragraph is not a smooth process. A lot of things can go wrong, but it works better than any other approach we know.

The job of the principal has become more overloaded, and vise-like, but at the same time the potential for playing a deeper and wider role is exciting. At this point, the upside possibilities are greater than the downside, not the least so because system coherence and cohesion cannot be effectively assessed without upgrading the role of the principal. There is a lot to fight for, so let's get down to it.

CHAPTER 6

Leading *WWFFP* into Action

In Frank Capra's 1939 film *Mr. Smith Goes to Washington*, James Stewart plays the part of a naïve bumpkin who ends up as a young senator. His father had given him this advice: "Remember, lost causes are the only things worth fighting for." *WWFFP* is not exactly about lost causes, but that is the spirit of it—relentless persistence in tackling tough issues. Recall the advice from surgeon Atul Gawande (2007), which exemplifies this same spirit: "in the absence of certainty, the truth is we want doctors who fight. . . . Always fight. Always look for what more you could do" (p. 159).

In *WWFFP* we want principals who fight! Guidelines for leading the fight have been interspersed throughout the previous five chapters, so I hope you already have considerable ammunition for the good fight. In this chapter I present a set of core guidelines—first for principals, then for system leaders. The main message, however, is for the principal: Lead the change you want to see.

GUIDELINES FOR PRINCIPALS

My six guidelines are:

1. De-privatize teaching.
2. Model instructional leadership.
3. Build capacity first.
4. Grow other leaders.
5. Divert the distractors.
6. Be a system leader.

I. De-Privatize Teaching

This is the biggest of the fights—to establish a culture in the teaching profession where it is normal and desirable for all teachers to observe and to be observed teaching. The norm of privacy has withstood decades of attempts to change it. John Goodlad and his colleagues wrote about it in *Behind the Classroom Door* in 1970. Dan Lortie, in *School Teacher* (1975), talked about the norm of teacher autonomy, along with conservatism and presentism, all of which amounted to keeping teaching relatively stagnant.

In the September 2007 issue of *Educational Leadership*, Susan Moore Johnson and Morgaen Donaldson document the "triple threat" that teacher leaders, such as literacy coaches, face: protecting autonomy, ensuring egalitarianism, and reinforcing seniority. Dan Lortie's findings are unchanged after a third of a century! This is not going to be easy.

De-privatizing teaching will require using all of our change knowledge. Here is a starter list:

- Declare de-privatization as the goal.
- Combine transparency (access to one another's teaching), nonjudgmentalism, and good help.
- Support teacher leaders (e.g., literacy coaches) in clarifying and legitimizing their roles, as well as in helping to develop their capacities.
- Hammer home a moral purpose, linked to instructional improvement and its causal connection to student achievement.
- Foster peer interaction without micromanaging it.

De-privatization is about transparency of practice. There is another aspect of transparency that is absolutely essential here, and that concerns *evidence-informed* decisionmaking. Instructional improvement must be continuous improvement. Therefore, we must always search for more effective pedagogical practices.

One of the most powerful instructional practices involves assessment literacy—the strategic use of data to improve teaching on a daily basis (assessment for learning), and the capacity to monitor results and engage the external accountability system. So de-privatization also means being transparent about student achievement. How well is the school doing? How well are individual teachers doing in moving the school forward? Student achievement data must be transparent to members of the staff and to the public, while protecting the school from data being used abusively (see *Secret Four—Transparency Rules* in Fullan, 2008).

We know that changes cannot be forced, but they can be pressed—directly by declaring the goal, and indirectly by using the peer culture. At the same time, use the other five guidelines in the service of explicitly de-privatizing teaching (see also Fullan, 2008).

Get in line with the other professions. Gawande (2007) quotes a leading medical reform: "to fix medicine we need to do two things: measure ourselves and be open about what we are doing" (p. 214). In short, to fix education, de-privatize it.

2. Model Instructional Leadership

The principal cannot be an instructional expert on every subject, but he or she can lead knowledgeably, as we have seen in Chapter 3. Modeling instruction means centering the school's mission around pedagogical improvements that result in student learning. Instructional leadership marshals all the school's resources to this end: budget, structure, professional learning, monitoring.

Such principals lead discussions on how well a school is progressing, and participate in many interactions, including attending workshops and sessions on capacity-building (Guideline 3). Principals must spend the bulk of their time engaged in instructional issues, delegating and diverting the distractions (Guideline 5).

Viviane Robinson's (2007) fine work defines school leadership as "identifying what works and why." What's worth fighting for is *precision and specificity* in modeling. Most advice to the principal on teaching instruction is too general. Robinson points out that "it is the combination of description, practical examples and theoretical explanation that makes for powerful professional learning" (p. 5).

Thus, modeling is not just symbolic. It is specific and concrete. Leithwood and colleagues (2007) and Robinson (2007) examined all the empirical studies they could find that linked instruction to student outcomes. They essentially arrived at the same conclusion. Some of it is about strategic direction, structure, and targeted resourcing, but more of it is about drilling down to specific actions. The largest effect (more than twice as significant as any other) that Robinson found concerned "promoting and participating in teacher learning and development," by which she meant "leadership that not only promotes, but directly participates with teachers in formal or informal professional learning" (p. 8). So, model instructional leadership, but model it with specificity—not with general symbolic stuff.

3. Build Capacity First

Capacity-building is the core route to improvement. It consists of new knowledge, skills, and competencies; additional resources (time, ideas, expertise, and money); and new motivation (the desire to put forth the effort to get results). If you want to change teachers, don't lecture them with moral purpose. Show them and enable them to find the way. I recommend avoiding *judgmentalism*, defined as "assessing something to be ineffective in a pejorative manner." Transparency does identify things that are ineffective. But if you want to change a situation, you must identify problems without stigmatizing the people experiencing them. As a change strategy, bullying backfires (Fullan, 2008).

Use capacity-building first because it is a better motivator. In fact, many teachers do not improve because they don't know how. Enabling the *how* is the key to forward movement. It doesn't mean the principal doesn't engage in judgment; it just means that it shouldn't be done prematurely. Yes, there are individual cases of unacceptable abuse or gross incompetence that must be acted on immediately, but for the vast majority of teachers, let capacity-building do its work.

Combine de-privatizing teaching, modeling of instruction, and capacity-building first, and you have a powerful force for change. Put another way, the pressure for change must be organic—built into the day-to-day culture of the school.

4. Grow Other Leaders

This is leading legacy today for tomorrow's sake, as we talked about in Chapter 2. If you know a lot as a leader, this is a tough one. It is often easier to do it yourself than to cultivate others who are less advanced than you are. On the flip side, it is difficult to lead others who are better at instruction than you are. But athletic coaches do this all the time. It is not sheer skill that matters, but a host of things that encompass "learning how to improve yourself," "working as a team member," "handling resistance," and so on.

Modeling instructional leadership, then, also means modeling what it looks like to help develop *other leaders*. Principals need to focus on instruction in all the ways we have been talking about, but they must do much of this through others. They do this, not by distant delegation, but by fostering coalescing leadership in which combinations of leaders are working together on instructional improvement. Pfeffer and Sutton (2006) put it best: "Perhaps the best way to view leadership is as a task of architecting organizational systems, teams, and cultures—as establishing the conditions and preconditions for others to succeed" (p. 200).

When you do this, you mobilize more power for the present to get the right things done, and you create a pipeline of future leaders who can carry on perhaps even more effectively than you—the best legacies have a touch of humility.

5. Divert the Distractors

Remember the PriceWaterhouseCoopers (2007) study of the principalship in England? They found that some school heads did the managerial operations work first, and if they had time left over, they led instruction (of course, they never had time left over); other heads reversed these priorities. This is the essence of Guideline 5.

But you can't let the school be managed in a shoddy fashion, either. Basically, the recommendation is that you take an explicit, proactive approach to managing the distractors. If you relate to distractors passively, they will rule you just about every day.

A combination of steps are needed. Take an inventory of operations, assign certain tasks to others, and make some tasks low or nonpriorities (recall the two guidelines in the original *WWFFP*)— "practice [selective] fearlessness," and "decide what you are not going to do"; let only the most urgent crises take you away from instruction.

If you practice the previous four guidelines, there will already be a lot of positive power pushing instruction to the fore. In addition, develop your own critical stance to the main distractors. Look to other principals in the system who seem to be able to focus on instruction, and make it a point to learn from them. The managerial area is where the system can help by investing directly in support for the operational work of the school (see System Guideline 5).

All and all, the practical demands of managerial and operational requirements are admittedly enormous, so this will not be an easy domain to master. But it is the kind of domain that, once you figure it out, it can keep paying dividends because it means that you are running a good school (poor management is itself an additional distractor) while you and the teachers concentrate on the main business of learning.

6. Be a System Leader

There is a selfish aspect to this guideline because it involves improving the outside context so that you will be better off, but there is also the altruistic obligation to help improve other schools and the system as a whole. Fortunately, the same actions can accomplish both of these goals simultaneously.

First, as we have seen in earlier chapters, it is in your best interests to be an active member in clusters or networks of schools, where you are learning from peers as well as contributing to their growth. Such networks can also help you develop your school culture internally, with teacher peers across schools modeling purposeful collaboration.

Second, a productive two-way relationship with district leaders is another way in which you can help improve the overall success of the district. District-wide reform is essential if there is to be individual school improvement on a continuous basis. Successful districts establish a "we–we" relationship between school and district leaders.

Third, as I have said earlier, the longevity of your school's success is severely undercut if you remain isolated, no matter how good the school becomes in the short run.

Finally, there are also bigger roles to play in the new models that are evolving, models in which "Executive Principals" have responsibility for more than one school, or where a struggling school is twinned with another school under the direction of a single principal (Munby, 2007).

All of this is compatible with Tim Brighouse's (2007) very helpful booklet in which he identifies the six tasks of leadership:

> Create energy
> Build capacity
> Meet and minimize crises
> Secure and enhance the environment
> Seek and chart improvement
> Extend the vision of what is possible

My message is to do this *systemically*—inside your own school, in relation to other schools, and for the system as a whole.

GUIDELINES FOR SYSTEMS

If principals pursue the six guidelines just discussed, it is tantamount to putting pressure on the larger system—the district and the state—to create the kind of infrastructure that complements the conditions for school success. If the larger system itself is proactive in this direction, all the better. Not only does that make it much more likely that you will be substantially supported in implementing the previous six guidelines, there also will be useful pressure from the outside for all schools to move in this direction. If this becomes the case, the chances of your colleagues in other schools becoming more helpful increases dramatically.

The system guidelines then complement or, in cases of limited school development, lead the fight for the principalship. Six guidelines reinforce the direction we have been pursuing in this book:

1. Elevate and invest in instructional leadership of the principal.
2. Combine direction and flexibility.
3. Mobilize the power of data.
4. Use peers to change district culture.
5. Address the managerial requirements.
6. Stay the course.

I. Elevate and Invest in the Instructional Leadership of the Principal

In general terms, this guideline means redefining the role of the principal as instructional leader, promoting people to the principalship on the basis of this role definition, enabling people to acquire experiences to meet the new criteria, using performance appraisals to reinforce the direction, and investing in capacity-building on the job.

But we don't have to be this general. We can look to and benchmark against systems that are doing this well. Consider the two that I introduced earlier: Boston Public Schools and York Region District in Ontario.

The McKinsey Report features Boston's program for developing principals (Barber & Mourshed, 2007). It consists of a three-pronged attack: a fellowship program, new principal support, and ongoing development. A few highlights are shown below:

Fellowship

- Three days a week working in schools with an experienced principal
- Two days a week in focused seminars on instructional leadership and management techniques
- Salary paid

New Principal Support

- Summer institute
- Mentoring
- Central support
- Network meetings
- Just-in-time sessions (covering specific problem areas as they arise)

Ongoing Development

- Deputy superintendents are required to spend most of their time coaching principals.
- Clusters: The district is divided into nine clusters of schools, each with a cluster leader who provides mentoring and support without having a direct evaluative or supervisory role (Barber & Mourshed, 2007).

York Region District (2007) has a "leadership development framework." This framework, like Boston's, provides a continuum of support and development, from emergent leadership, to first-time administrators, to experienced leadership (required training for vice principals and principals). York's development approach is totally congruent with the ideas expressed in *WWFFP*. It is based on coaching, mentoring, network learning, and cross-level learning initiatives specific to instruction (such as literacy and numeracy). Their framework encompasses four leadership competency domains: setting directions and sustaining vision, building relationships, leading and managing instruction, and further developing the organization. Within these domains there is a suite of required training activities, along with self-directed professional learning, where principals select certain competencies that they want to develop.

Boston and York Region exemplify Guideline 1. They integrate instruction and leadership development.

2. Combine Direction and Flexibility

Effective districts are aware of and manage the too-tight/too-loose dilemma. The other five guidelines all feed into this guideline, so I will be brief here. There needs to be direction: identifying certain non-negotiable goals pertaining to literacy and numeracy and, equally, developing the most effective instructional practices, which should become less negotiable as they become more proven. But if you get too prescriptive, you squeeze out creativity, passion, and commitment. Therefore, local-school leeway is an essential ingredient. It is possible, and indeed essential, to combine precision (relentless consistency in applying effective methods) with creativity (searching for innovative ways of improving performance and results).

The best way of expressing this guideline is to say that, when it works, school leaders and district leaders feel that they are pursuing a jointly determined agenda. There is no "we–they" division. The agendas mesh. Shared goals are combined for the good of all schools. Each school has its own distinctive version, suitable to its own particular context. Vertical and horizontal sharing and two-way communication sort out a lot of differences and enable people to converge on common effective practices. Where there are differences, they are known and understood, if not always appreciated.

Leaders at both school and district levels are wary of both ends of the continuum: too-tight authoritarianism (whether through a dominant leader or an equally domineering "group-think" by peers) or the laissez-faire drift of a thousand flowers looking to bloom.

3. Mobilize the Power of Data

I have already emphasized in the principals' guidelines that data on student learning—daily data used as assessment strategies for learning, and longitudinal data on whether the school is on the move—represent a crucial component that serves simultaneously as a strategy for immediate improvement and as an instrument of internal and external accountability.

Here is where the district must help in two ways. First, by setting up the technologies that makes the acquisition and availability of data efficient, timely, and easy. It is hard enough for principals to work with teachers on the actual use of data for improvement without having to spend valuable time accessing it and trying to decipher its literal meaning. Thus, a large part of the technical burden must be borne by the district infrastructure. The second way the district must help is through training school leaders in how to use information for data-informed decisionmaking. This is a key capacity that the district must foster in all of its developmental actions. Districts need to promote transparency while playing down judgmentalism.

4. Use Peers to Change District Culture

The district doesn't have to do all the direct work in refashioning the role of the principal. It can multiply its efforts more powerfully through stimulating purposeful peer interaction among principals. In the same way that principals can improve school culture through fostering peer exchanges among teachers and between teachers and teacher leaders, central leaders can best affect district culture by basing strategies on focused exchanges across schools.

None of these guidelines stands alone. There is plenty of direction coming from Guidelines 1–3. Let the principals interact to do the work of processing many of the ideas generated through the other guidelines.

5. Address the Managerial Requirements

This is a very specific requirement. If there is one concrete change that I would recommend in the face of the growing instructional *and* managerial demands on the principalship, it would be to find specific, efficient ways to address the less important of the two demands. This is both practical and doable.

First, training and capacity-building should be provided to assist principals in handling the managerial side of the role— plant, personnel, finance, personal health and safety. Strategies for delegation and efficient management can be identified and developed, as Boston and York Region are doing with their principals.

Second, and more radical at first glance, is to create, train, and certify the new role of "business manager": one full-time business manager per school for large schools, and, for small schools, one per three to five schools. Thus, a powerful step forward entails the creation of the new role of business manager, who works under the supervision of the principal to take care of the distractors through professional management. There may be other ways of addressing this goal, such as enhancing the role of assistant principals, but, whatever the case, the solution must explicitly define the required resources.

I don't mean that resources should be doled out on a mere formulaic basis. The whole phenomenon has to be approached carefully and incrementally so that the work is done by skilled managers and the relationship of the business manager to the principal is made clear. The English, as we have seen, have done exactly this in fairly short order on a pilot basis. And I reported earlier that an external evaluation of the program showed substantial per-student savings, along with an increase in resources through the efforts of the principal and the business manager working as a team (Munby, 2007).

This is one of those obvious high-yield strategies that courageous state and district leaders should take by the horns. The school leader's role as instructional leader is hard enough without it being hampered unnecessarily. Make the principal the CEO, not the all-purpose superwoman/man.

6. Stay the Course

If there is anything that makes teachers and principals cynical about change, it is the constant flip-flop of direction that happens when superintendents come and go. School boards, as some have observed, seem to cycle in and out of episodic "policy churns"! The politics of the day seem to conspire to produce periodic shifts that are either aimless or, more often, divorced from current or previous priorities.

Successful systems focus on a small number of critical, ambitious goals, and then stay the course. Some districts are discovering this. Both Boston and York Region have been successful because they have focused on the right areas, and then stayed with them. The top-performing countries, states, and provinces in the world do the same thing (Barber & Mourshed, 2007). In so doing, these systems have profoundly embedded these priorities and corresponding effective practices into their cultures across all levels—school, district, government.

Such systems have done this through a decade of continuity and a deepening of good direction. At the district level, this has involved the same superintendent working with a school board that understood continuity and depth. Both Boston and York Region have, or will have in the near future, new superintendents; because of the embedded culture, it is a good bet that these systems will continue and deepen their chosen course. You don't have to have the same person leading year after year, but you do need to select for "planned continuity" of good direction.

Few things prepare teachers and principals to focus on quality and continuous innovation than having a district that knows and supports a district-wide enterprise of instructional improvement for moral purpose.

I have not set out a corresponding third set of guidelines for the governmental level, but we have been doing just that in working with certain state-level politicians and policymakers. Ontario, for example, has made substantial strides in the past 4 years by focusing on a small number of goals, setting targets jointly with districts on literacy and numeracy, investing in capacity-building, creating a usable database, intervening nonpejoratively, and so on (Fullan, 2007, Ch. 12).

WWFFP REVISITED

This is the 20th anniversary of the original publication of *WWFFP*. Have we made any headway? It's been slow. But compared to the first publication, the current one is less general, more targeted and specific, and more able to point to concrete examples in the field that reflect the new agenda. There is more impatience with the status quo and with the current lack of progress. There is more openness and more of a sense of urgency to act. And more kindred spirits are engaged in the action. Above all, the principalship is being recognized by *all* as truly critical in importance.

The encouraging news is that much of this action has occurred in the past 5 years, and is accelerating in 2008. The new ideas are radical, with great power and potential to transform the system. Maybe the slow part has been laying the foundation for takeoff. If so, this is an exciting time to be, or to contemplate being, a school leader. Maybe what's worth fighting for is not just the lost causes, but the chance to make the new opportunities a reality. Lead the change you want to see.

References

Abrahamson, E. (2004). *Change without pain*. Boston: Harvard Business School Press.

Barber, M., & Mourshed, M. (2007). *How the world's best-performing school systems come out on top*. London: McKinsey and Company.

Black, P., Harrison, C., Lee, C., Marshal, B., & Wiliam, D. (2003). *Assessment for learning*. Philadelphia: Open University Press.

Brighouse, T. (2007). *How successful head teachers thrive and survive*. London: RM. Available at www.rn.com/successfulheads

Caldwell, B. (2006). *Re-imagining educational leadership*. Melbourne, Australia: Australian Council for Educational Research.

Collins, J. (2001). *Good to great*. New York: HarperCollins.

Cross City Campaign for Urban School Reform. (2005). *A delicate balance: District policies and classroom practice*. Chicago: Author.

Dufour, R., Dufour, R., Eaker, R., & Many, T. (2006). *Learning by doing: A handbook for professional learning communities at work*. Bloomington, IN: Solution Tree.

Elmore, R. (2000). *Building a new structure for school leadership*. Washington, DC: Albert Shanker Institute.

Elmore, R. (2004). *School reform from the inside out: Policy, practice and performance*. Cambridge, MA: Harvard University Press.

Friedman, T. (2005). *The world is flat*. New York: Farrar, Straus and Giroux.

Fullan, M. (1997). *What's worth fighting for in the principalship?* New York: Teachers College Press. (Original work published 1988)

Fullan, M. (2006). *Turnaround leadership*. San Francisco: Jossey-Bass.

Fullan, M. (2007). *The new meaning of educational change* (4th ed.). New York: Teachers College Press.

Fullan, M. (2008). *The six secrets of change: How leaders survive and thrive*. San Francisco: Jossey-Bass.

Fullan, M., & Hargreaves, A. (1996). *What's worth fighting for in your school?* New York: Teachers College Press.

Fullan, M., Hill, P., & Crévola, C. (2006). *Breakthrough.* Thousand Oaks, CA: Corwin.

Gawande, A. (2007) *Better: A surgeon's notes on performance.* New York: Metropolitan Books.

Goodland, J., Klein, M., & Associates. (1970). *Behind the classroom door.* Worthington, OH: Charles Jones.

Haidt, J. (2006). *The happiness hypothesis.* New York: Basic Books.

Hargreaves, A., & Fink, D. (2006) *Sustainable leadership,* San Francisco: Jossey-Bass.

Hargreaves, A., & Fullan, M. (1998). *What's worth fighting for out there?* New York: Teachers College Press.

Hargreaves, D., & Shirley, D. (2006). *The long and short of school improvement: Final report, RATL project.* Boston: Boston College.

Heifetz, R., & Linsky, M. (2002). *Leadership on the line.* Boston: Harvard Business School Press.

Hubbard, L., Mehan, H., & Stein, M. K. (2006). *Reform as learning.* London: Routledge.

Jersey Public School (2007, June). *The literacy journey at Jersey Public School.* Presentation at The Learning Fair, Richmond Hill, York Region Public District School Board.

Johnson, S. M., & Donaldson, M. (2007). Overcoming obstacles to leadership. *Educational Leadership, 65*(1), 8–13.

Kruse, S., Louis, K., & Bryk, A. (1995) *Building professional learning in schools.* Madison, WI: Center on Organization and Restructuring of Schools.

Leithwood, K., Louis, K., Anderson, S., & Wahlstrom, K. (2004). *How leadership influences student learning.* New York: The Wallace Foundation.

Leithwood, K., Dry, C., Sammons, P., Harris, A., & Hopkins, D. (2007) *Seven strong claims abut successful school leadership.* Nottingham, England: National College of School Leadership.

Liker, J., & Meier, D. (2007). *Toyota talent.* New York: McGraw Hill.

Little, J. W. (1981). The power of organizational setting. Paper adapted from the final report *School success and staff development.* Washington, DC: National Institute of Education.

Lortie, D. (1975). *School teacher.* Chicago: University of Chicago Press.

Marzano, R., (2007). *The art and science of teaching.* Alexandria, VA: Association for Supervision and Curriculum Development.

McLaughlin, M., & Talbert, J. (2006). *Building school-based teacher learning communities.* New York: Teachers College Press.

Minthrop, H. (2004). *Schools on probation.* New York: Teachers College Press.

Mintzberg, H. (2004). *Managers not MBAs.* San Francisco: Berrett-Koehler.

Munby, S. (2007, June). Speech to the National College of School Leadership's Seizing Success Conference, Nottingham, England.

New York City Schools. (2006). *Children first: A bold commonsense plan to create great schools.* New York: Author.

Nye, B., Konstantopoulus, S., & Hedges, L. (2004). How large are teacher effects? *Educational Evaluation and Policy Analysis, 26*(3), 237–257.

Pfeffer, J., & Sutton, R. (2006). *Hard facts, dangerous half truths, and total nonsense: Profiting from evidence-based management.* Boston: Harvard Business School Press.

PriceWaterhouseCoopers. (2007). *An independent study of the headship.* London: Author.

Robinson, V. (2007). *School leadership and student outcomes: Identifying what works and why.* Sydney: Australian Council of Educational Leadership.

Robinson, V., Hohepa, M., & Lloyd, C. (2007). *School leadership and student outcomes, Identifying what works and why: A best evidence synthesis iteration.* Wellington, New Zealand: Ministry of Education.

Rosenholtz, S. (1989). *Teachers' workplace.* New York: Longman.

Sharratt, L., & Fullan, M. (2006). Accomplishing districtwide reform. *Journal of School Leadership, 16*(5), 583–595.

Shaw, G. B. (1903). *Man and superman.* Cambridge, UK: Cambridge University Press.

Shirley, D., & Hargreaves, A. (2006). Data driven to distraction. *Education Week, 26*(6), 32–33.

Sisodia, R., Wolfe, D., & Sheth, J. (2007). *Firms of endearment: How world-class companies profit from passion and purpose.* Upper Saddle River, NJ: Wharton School Publishing.

Thornhill Secondary School. (2007, June). *Strengthening our literacy foundation.* Presentation at The Learning Fair, Richmond Hill, York Region District School Board.

Wallace Foundation. (2003). *Beyond the pipeline.* New York: Author.

About the Author

Michael Fullan is Professor Emeritus at the Ontario Institute for Studies in Education at the University of Toronto, and is Special Adviser on Education to Dalton McGuinty, the Premier of Ontario.

Fullan is a doer and thinker. He served as Dean of the Faculty of Education at the University of Toronto from 1988 to 2003, leading two major organizational transformations including a merger of two large schools of education. He is currently working as adviser–consultant on several major education reform initiatives around the world.

Michael Fullan bases his work on the moral purpose of education as it is applied in schools and school systems to bring about major improvements. He has written several best sellers that have been translated into many languages.

His most recent book is *The Six Secrets of Change*.

Visit his website at www.michaelfullan.ca